Raag Leaves
for
Paresh Chakraborty

Andrew Brewerton

Shearsman Books
Exeter

Published in the United Kingdom in 2008 by
Shearsman Books Ltd
58 Velwell Road
Exeter EX4 4LD

www.shearsman.com

ISBN   978-1-905700-78-3

Copyright © Andrew Brewerton, 2008.

The right of Andrew Brewerton to be identified as the author of this work has been asserted by him in accordance with the Copyrights, Designs and Patents Act of 1988. All rights reserved. No part of this publication may be reproduced, stored in a retrieval system, transmitted in any form or by any means, electronic, mechanical, photocopying, recording or otherwise, without the prior permission of the publisher.

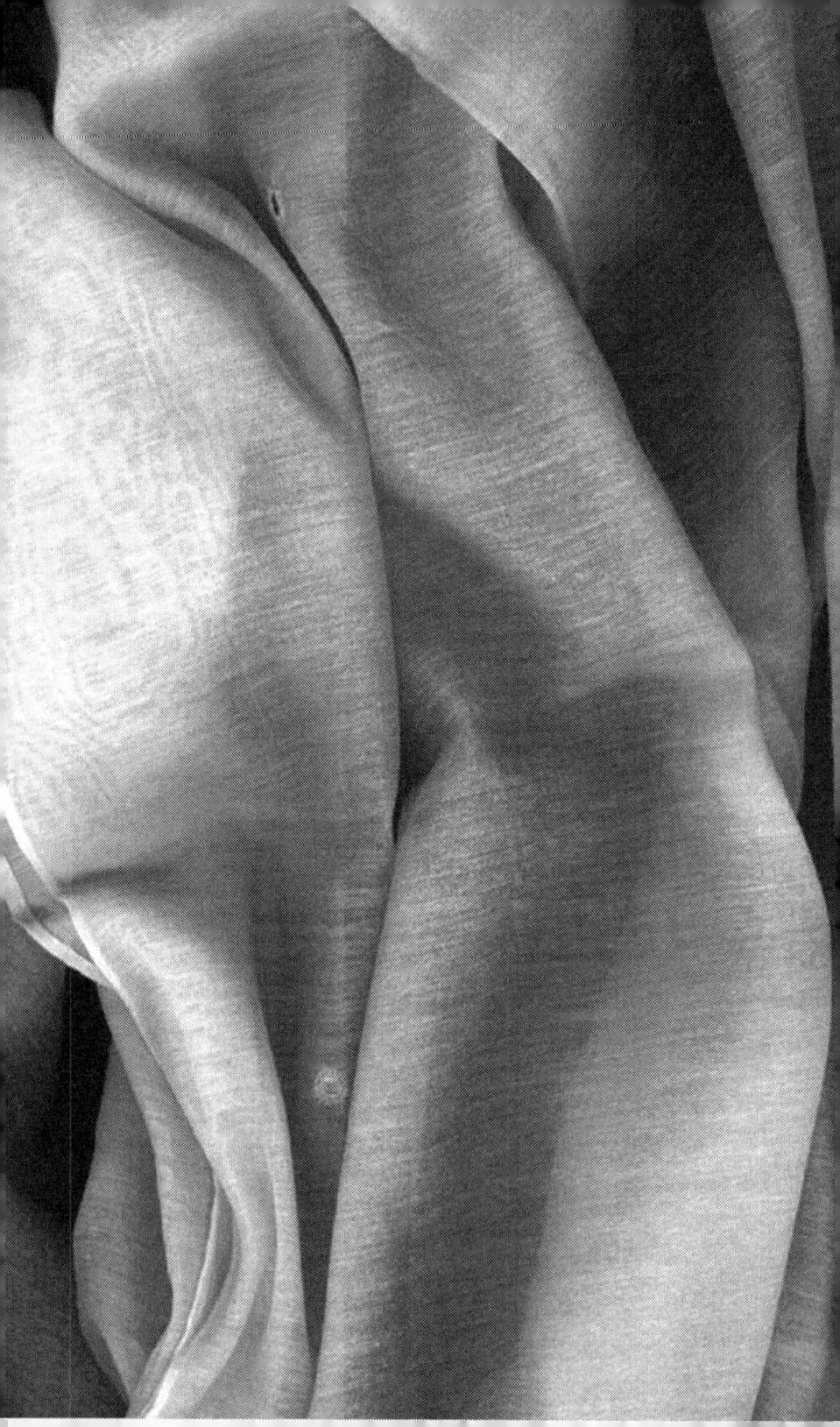

যচ্ছেদ্ বাঙ্‌মনসী প্রাজ্ঞস্তদ্ যচ্ছেজ্‌জ্ঞান আত্মনি।
জ্ঞানমাত্মনি মহতি নিযচ্ছেৎ তদ্যচ্ছেচ্ছান্ত আত্মনি॥ ১৩

উত্তিষ্ঠত জাগ্রত
প্রাপ্য বরান্ নিবোধত।
ক্ষুরস্য ধারা নিশিতা দুরত্যয়া
দুর্গং পথস্তৎ কবয়ো বদন্তি॥ ১৪

Supriya

1962 – 2006

Raag
Leaves
for
Paresh
Chakraborty

Certains mourraient de soif – entre une carafe d'eau et une tasse à café.

Braque, *Cahier*

Uneven the ground is
instrumental   walking range
these briar roads all chance
impediment   *that's*
its sound   the foot
hills   accompanied
distance   *its voice*
opened there

           so depending on
cold feet trail in cinder   glass scree
kicked traces turned   to bracken ash
feet falling   ling sintered   impressions
foundering   sand   pearl ash
on lead   brick red to char
coal unearthly   *down this long road*
without his soul being covered

              or lifts like slip
shod in clay milk   a glaze
with standing   waters   laced
guttered light   you'd play to your
clay content   depending
where you fall now   out of your way
of course   *just here*   she said and
              here

             touch
sleeps in its course   a flushed reed
descanting   threaded sound   files
in thin continuity   *a kinde of staide*
musicke   vessel   now & then
communicating waters   this broken road
soaked & loaded   only to release
a line drawn to   touch

      sleeping moth to leaf   curled
the drawn night together   imagined
simple materials   a brush stroke
resin   smoke releasing   a wolf
from pine wood   ventures her inkling
shadow   our figures drawn on raw
silk ground   tonight   no paper trails
our knowing   unanswerable light

        gathering iron   a resting
angle of incidence   as a soft push
breaking glass skin   bright markings
moving   in the ring   in a quickening
clockwise gather   fire lizard   lifts
to shed her molten tail   flow back
tap up and marver   out of thin air
acquiring   tempered scales

sleep   walk   a slip
road in   slender rain   your coat of milk-
glass   dew these early hours   adrift
in your waking   cupped to lip   stroke on
stroke   your swimming forms
upstream of me   *coiling dragons*
in various positions   playing pearl
among waves and clouds

      nothing stirs   this sonority
of voices in the wood   the soft drum
in your throat   pulse   this pressing
timbre   arches tree high   to damp
in foiled   acoustic   shading overtones
we lip-synch   part song   a new leaf
touch   so close   your heart   prints
                my heart

plunge pool   over the wrist slipt
ice lit   noose of water   takes
my hand away   streaming hand
to mouth taken in   drinks in the hollow
of its making   open gifts pour
through thin   skin my emptying
hands   flying white   *without haste*
and without rest

   so reeling out our time is
that straine agen wound in
outdistancing light *a falling figure*
in the strings feint line played in
shadow configured *like you were*
walking in the air Ida's dream high
pagoda so drawn we go truth lies
in being just so

                      grass harp   a blade
vane   strung thumb hollows   answers
a goose   in a dead language   asthma
wind blown   uncertain   whence my next breath will
come   Brahma   blows his nose   for the goose
is language   and of Brahma   *who alone is true*
utter   and omnific   so what   do you say
what part then   does speaking play

           local colour   look
looks this way   located   looks itself
up & down   where   changed   your eye
takes you   shot   with azure   inner
colour   a sleeve of still   water   surveillance
echoes location   where   a crystal eye
well   a wheel rut   pools   and you are
taken   your gaze away

chorale

            affect benevolent   cynical
definitely   effect fallacious
gregarious hyperbole   irony   jaded
karma   love   metaphor naïve
oxymoron   paradox   quixotic rhetoric
sex theme ubiquitous   virtue
whether   xenophobia   yield
                              zeal

light catches   like
blown graphite   grainy   draws your eye
in a negative snow cast   wintering light in shadow
scree   pictures   the news   a spilt figure   blood
proof   boot stamp blood   shed in snow   some
rearguard mandate that was   *it was neither*
a staying nor a going   says the diplomat   *just*
a quiet reduction   to safe areas

          the graves   unsugared under
sweet immersion   uncured tissue   and twisted
over   no meadow sweet   or rushes growing
but wheatfields   corn silk drifting   all the same
all clothed in   paper clay rags   *how long to gather*
all the remains   he thought for a minute
their faces   their arms and legs   *my grandchildren*
could be doing this

        rising and falling so   how
we make the night   crossing   shear
water   shaving lint away   to tidal black
to tiding brine   plied   undressing
a water lesion   ferried   in the entire
province of Monday night   rising and falling
silent   straitened   a slipped line
outplaying time

sonorous air   nothing
more or less   above this stream's each move
and new device   cutting siltstone
brushes the acoustic curtain   *do not climb*
the waterfall   hand touching hand   held in
uncertain scaling   *please move through*
quickly and quietly   hand to mouth
rare birds are nesting in this area

      what isn't there   that can't be
taken in   a moment   looking up
from working   out of doors   in a landscape
figured standing   eyebright   in the verge
of here and there   Doug what are you
doing here   with your fair eyes   stolen
upon me   a moment   in that sheer
transparency   unless

                in a landscape   damsons
blue underfoot   blue to white   *nebbi'*
a la valle   and glancing up   a late rose
opens somewhere   making room   shuttering
crystal   lights an olive distance   slope
of whitish ground   *e nebbi' a la muntagne*
in the open   olive fall   a walk among trees
& stript leaves   a stray line   *ne la campagna*

        nen ce sta nesciune   for you lose
yourself   outer   out of kilter   cut to
mislaid   a stone path rising   forgetting verges
giving ground   a stream of leaving   *addije
addije amore*   cut to   an olive grove
cut down   so we gather   *casch'e se coje*
gathered in   a ruinous quick look back   *la live
e casch' a l'albere li foje*

*there were more olive trees then
where the pines are   there were no pines
here yes   this is where it was   maybe
a bit further up   a bit further down   but
here   this is where it was   there were
far more olive trees   but they rooted them out
to plant the pines   the pines are recent
there was nothing here*

             what isn't there   that can't be
taken in   a moment   looking up
from working   out of doors   in a landscape
figured standing   speedwell   in the verge
of here and there   Doug what are you
doing here   with your fair eyes   stolen
upon me   a moment   in that sheer
transparency   unless

            lampblack
ochre   orpiment   indigo   green silver
colour   for outlines   the body beneath
clinging   garments   colloid of tin
cheap   and unlike silver   did not lose
its lustre   after burnishing   modelling
of form   with darker tones   applied
        to a wet paper surface

                    how she folds
    the note   holds it over   the implication
    of time   in time   loosening furl
    on fold   an open timbre   slowed
    to a rhythm   tone over tone   successive
    thresholds   slip by in this   her shaken
    grace   opens the night colours   all the time
    she takes   for love

            night   an open window
  star   light dilating   milk   across
  a lacquer table   your form there your look   *quand*
  nos yeux se touchent   fait-il jour   ou fait-il
  nuit   you moving only   slightly your lips
  parted slender   reclining   the long night cool
  in lit shellac   & I am still in this   this visitation
  you   only you

*the sky was lit up
with a bright yellow   light the earth
appeared   white   the yellow gradually
became   darker turning   gradually
to orange   in the sky I saw white
clouds   the sand is brown   the glaze
is bright green   it is a wonderful sight
from the air*

                              once
more   and again   our time   this day even
today   *they are killing the children*   Da'ud
many children   *killed*   thus   here
& now then   lies   their peace ever
lasting   under stone scree   screened life laid out
before gigantic armour   *they make a desert*
and they call it peace

                        thus is this
fulfilment   David   cut out in   self figuring
slaughter   so tall you stand   amongst the philistines
your limbs so   disproportionate   & heavy
handed   your swollen head   from stone released
and perfect   lifted high into the air   as these too
rise as smoke   and dust like   a desert
storm   adrift   in their asymmetry

                          ingrained in
every white detail   unblinking   looks clothed
in concrete rime   small coated figures   shadows taken
out   trailing print columns   unbecoming   from sky
to sky   still their voices now   *of the most elusive*
register   sounds like grief   soar   above the psalmist
high and thin   *like finest muslin*   it will not
wash

                    a strip of gauze
unwinding   diesel fabric   coarse day
light fibres   loosely bound   a stone's
throw   from there   *but there*   *is a path*
even to that distance   vertiginous   given the lie
of the land   *beyond words*   choking song
throat burns   and gags   stop your mouth
with rags

                      mauve   *this colour*
      lacked permanence   manganese blue
      pigment now unavailable   rose madder
      alizarin   *close*   *to alizarin*
      crimson   vermilion   *bright red*
      pigment now unavailable   chrome
      yellow   *toxicity*   *and lack*
      of permanence   discontinued colours

       as yet   still   a moment
remaining   every frame it is   for you this quality
like lichen   take it   clean from thin air   *nature
morte*   dead still   alive   to this   the frost
pursues its sacred tendency   to description
unhindered   being   a waiting on still   even
now mid flow   to step & not step   you are and you are
again

    unstill   my sleeping fault
line rising   inliered   to breaking clay
measures   the long mynd come to
unanswering light   so springs abound
young stream   in its cadence   declining
an infinitive present   in water inscribes
a *vocalise* with stone tact   all spilt
notation   a murmur   arranging its bed

touching so
to speak   phænomenal distance   *what is there
here*   slips between here   and there   horizons
edges   bed   to table coffee   cup water   jug
glass open   window outside   tall hedgerow   insects
scaling slant evening light   new moon unseen   all this
thirsting   after presence   in your eyes   love
making touching so   stripped thread   bare melody

       something and
nothing where this emptiness is itself
exhausted wastes no shred remains
of emptiness fullness how much
is this visual where there is this little
very thin ribbon of light no there there
there is no horizon *and there is*
    no colour

        incised luminous   a skull
doubles   as a palette   another   one last
coat   their familiar   always   *raw*
umber   *burnt*   *umber*   *raw*   *sienna*
burnt sienna   *yellow*   *ochre lamp*
black   *vine*   *black*   *bone*   *black*
ultramarine   *orange-yellow*   *antimony*
        yellow

        so eyes resting then
against the sometime   open wall
of light   pauses   all that we are
close with   the moist afternoon
beads our skin   all open pored
inward   held in   your slow crescent
curve   these printed sheets   our little
given heat.

The wise one should offer up speech and mind:
He should offer it up into the conscious soul.
He should offer up the knowing into the great soul:
He should offer that up into the peaceful soul.

Stand up! Wake up!
[. . .]
This is a difficult path,
A razor's sharp edge, hard to cross –
So the poets say.

Kaṭha Upaniṣad, III (13-14), adapted from *The Upaniṣads*, translated and edited by Valerie J. Roebuck, revised edition (Penguin Books, 2003) pp. 282-3. Chosen by my friend Paresh Chakraborty, in the way of dedication and epigraph. The original Sanskrit verses appear on page 5.

Notes

The epigraph by Braque on page 13 translates as *Some would die of thirst between a jug of water and a coffee cup*. (*Cahier de Georges Braque, 1916-1947*. Maeght éditeur, Paris, 1994, p. 59.)

The phrase *"quand nos yeux se touchent, fait-il jour ou fait-il nuit"* (when our eyes meet, is it day or is it night?) in the poem *'night an open window'* derives from Jacques Derrida.

The five-poem sequence *'what isn't there'; 'in a landscape'; 'nen ce sta nesciune'; 'there were more olive trees', and 'what isn't there'* was published as *Cade l'uliva*, an elegy for Douglas Oliver (Poetical Histories, Cambridge 2003).

'Cade l'uliva' is the title of a traditional work song of the *magnarelle*, or olive-gatherers, of the Plain of Ortona below the mountain of the Maiella in Abruzzo, Italy:

> *Mist in the valley, cloud up on the mountain.*
> *In all the landscape, not a soul.*
> *So long, so long my love*
> *We fall and are gathered.*
> *The olives are fallen, the trees are stript of leaves.*

[Ref. *Bella Ciao. Chansons du peuple en italie. Il nuovo canzoniere italiano* (*Musique d'abord* series, Harmonia Mundi, 2000. HMA 195734) tracks 3 and 27]

The recorded song is unaccountably omitted from *Canti Popolari Abruzzese, raccolti da Emiliano Giancristoforo* (Quaderni di Rivista Abruzzese, n° 42, 2002) ISBN 88-88340-42-4, though cited (p.89) in a 1975 transcription by P. Donatangelo Lupinetti as CD2/track 17.

The fourth stanza *'there were more olive trees'* derives *in toto* from the testimony of 'M.C.', cited in Ian Gibson (1883). *The Assassination of Federico García Lorca* (Harmondsworth, Penguin Books) p. 165.

'The sky was lit up' derives from a letter by Richard P. Feynman to his mother, Lucille Feynman, dated August 9th, 1945, published in *Don't You Have Time To Think?* edited by Michelle Feynman (London, Allen Lane, 2005) pp. 65-8.

Some of these poems have been published, as they appear here or in earlier drafts, by *Poetical Histories*; *The Gig*; *Two Entangled Events*; *CCCP16*; and */seconds*; and performed variously in London, Cambridge, Dartington and at Furzeacres on Dartmoor. An elegy for Douglas Oliver was published as *Cade l'uliva* (Poetical Histories, 2004), and *Da'ud* can be found at www.slashseconds.org. Some recorded materials are also accessible at www.archiveofthenow.org, and at www.wildhoneypress.com. The author's thanks go especially to Peter Riley, Chris Goode, Nate Dorward, Paige Mitchell, Sam Ladkin, Josh Robinson, Kevin and Lesley Nolan, Philip Kuhn and Rosie Musgrave, Derek Horton, to Andrea Brady, and to Randolph Healy, for these things.

www.ingramcontent.com/pod-product-compliance
Lightning Source LLC
Chambersburg PA
CBHW031200160426
43193CB00008B/457